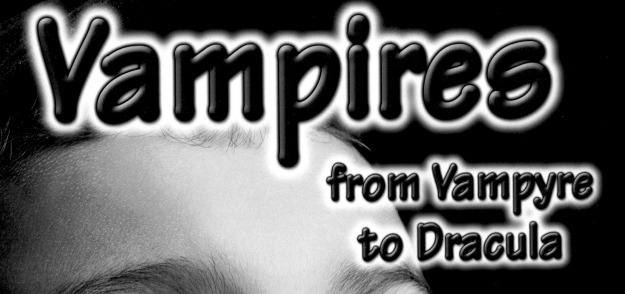

Vampires
from Vampyre
to Dracula

Dr Brian Knapp

Contents

The terror of darkness

Many people have a fascination with vampires. Most enjoy reading horror stories or watching creepy films of vampires. Some people even believe vampires really exist. But what is the background to the vampire story, why are we fascinated by it, and where does the idea of a vampire come from? To understand that, we first need to look at ourselves.

People have always worried about things they did not understand or things they had no control over. Most especially, people have worried about what happens when you are dead and whether you can come alive again in some way. People also worry about the dark, because then our eyes do not let us see clearly much of what goes on. Nocturnal animals have a big advantage over us in the dark. So we feel scared of things that might attack us suddenly. Bats, for example, fly about very quickly at night using ultrasound to guide them.

All we glimpse is a dark shadow flitting past us. Spiders might entangle us in giant webs – the list of things that frighten us goes on.

To help us see in the dark, people shine lights: street lights today and fires in the past. Fire – light – thus becomes a symbol of good, while dark is a symbol of evil.

A sense of evil

If people want to do evil things, they most often do them at night. They camouflage themselves with dark clothes. They move in the shadows. In this way, black becomes a symbol of evil and, of course, white is a symbol of goodness.

Our most precious thing is our blood. Giving our blood is a sacrifice, but having it taken from us forcibly is a terrible sign of evil – or so we think.

We like to feel comfortable and safe. We feel less safe in surroundings or with people we do not know. Mysterious foreigners or the thought of foreign places can be unsettling.

We are at our most defenceless when we are held against our

will, such as in a prison. Castles have been used as prisons for centuries. They have high towers and strong gates. And no-one really knows what goes on inside their forbidding walls.

Above all, we are afraid of people who seem to be kind and friendly but who really have evil deeds in mind. Victorian mothers, for example, would warn their children that if they did something wrong the 'Bogey Man' would get them.

So our own fears create images in our minds of darkness, blackness, blood, double-dealing and being defenceless.

Welcome to the world of vampires...

Return of the undead

Because no-one knows what happens when we die, there is always a fear of the unknown.

What happens if we do not die? This fear of being undead is made more dramatic because nobody likes looking in a coffin and seeing a rotted corpse. But what if the corpse were not rotted, but still had flesh, with growing fingernails and teeth, and with blood dripping from the mouth? That is truly terrifying.

Scientists will tell you that corpses often change that way before they finally decompose, and some kinds of coffins make decomposing a very slow process. But for those who are less knowledgeable, the idea of the undead can become fearful.

The vampire – one of the undead – becomes a night creature, a demon of the dark. It can only move about at night and must return to its coffin before daybreak.

Vampire sightings

The idea of the undead can be found in writings as old as those from Ancient Egypt and Ancient Greece. The first vampire records in Britain go back to the 13th century.

But it is in Eastern Europe that most vampire records are found. In late medieval times, there are records of dead peasants who were later seen alive. Panic set in among villagers when it was reported that the undead were drinking blood. It was clearly time for urgent action: first by driving a stake through their hearts, and if this did not stop the sightings, then they were

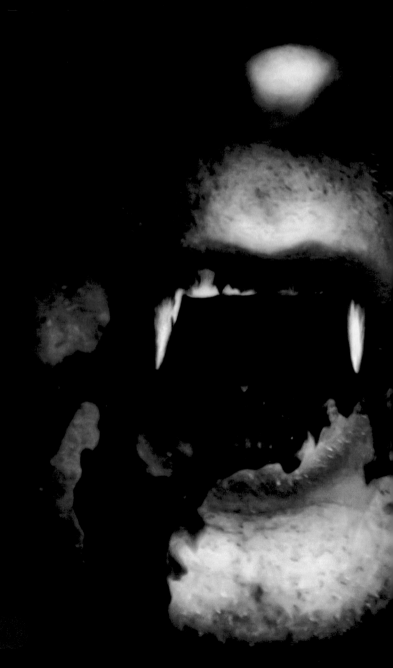

beheaded and their hearts taken out and burned.

This was not just something believed by ignorant peasants, but also by many learned people. In the 18th century, famous writer Voltaire wrote, "These vampires were corpses, who went out of their graves at night to suck the blood of the living, either at their throats or stomachs, after which they returned to their cemeteries. The persons so sucked waned, grew pale, and fell into consumption; while the sucking corpses grew fat, got rosy, and enjoyed an excellent appetite."

Spread of the legend

The modern idea of vampires spread from Eastern Europe, the lands whose ancestors were Slavs. In the days before Christianity, Slav religions focused on ancestor worship and household spirits.

The ancient Slavs believed that the soul could not be killed with the body. They believed that upon death the soul would go out of the body and wander for 40 days before moving on to the afterlife. During this time the soul could re-enter its dead body.

The ancient Slavs believed that some spirits were good and could help people, while others were harmful and came from ancestors or dead people.

From this ancient religious idea came the vampire: an evil undead spirit which needs the blood of the living to keep its dead body from decomposing.

As books began to be written on superstitions from the East, so knowledge of vampires spread. Then, as people emigrated from Eastern Europe, so these superstitions migrated with them, so that even in the 19th century it was quite common for Americans to believe in vampires.

Many stories spread from the wild mountainous regions of Eastern Europe. Superstitions tend to be strongest in isolated communities.

Gothic Horror

Vampire stories are part of a kind of writing called Gothic Horror, where you have a mixture of young lovers and terror created by the evil, middle-aged nobleman who wants to carry away the fair maid.

It is called Gothic Horror because it is often set in ancient medieval buildings whose style is known as Gothic. The Gothic writers thought that medieval buildings were dark and mysterious and connected with what they saw as a dark and terrifying period of harsh laws and torture. To them, the medieval period had mysterious, fantastic and superstitious rituals. So writers introduced terror, mystery, ghosts, haunted houses, castles, darkness, death, decay, madness, secrets and hereditary curses.

The main characters of Gothic fiction could be anyone who caused terror or mayhem: insane maniacs, wicked professors and doctors, werewolves, skeletons, zombies and, of course – vampires. All this took place in castles (preferably

partly ruined), monasteries, old large houses and ancient burial sites such as graveyards.

The first Gothic Horror book was probably 'The Castle of Otranto' published in 1764 and written by Horace Walpole. This, and later novels written in the same way, were immediate best-sellers.

A modern drawing of the classic vampire story.

The first vampire story

The first vampire story, called 'The Vampyre', was a short story by John William Polidori published in a magazine on the 1st of April 1819. It was the first time a figure from folklore had been made into a whole new way of writing. It is a horror story.

Its characters are Lord Ruthven – an attractive, middle-aged British nobleman of mysterious origins. He is the vampire. Aubrey, who is a young gentleman, is the hero. Ianthe, who is a beautiful woman Aubrey meets on his journeys with Ruthven.

We know exactly how this story came about. Making up ever-more exaggerated stories was the fashionable craze among the writers of the time. John Polidori was staying in Italy with famous literary people Lord Byron and Percy Bysshe Shelley and his wife Mary Shelley. The companions were kept indoors by rainy weather and they began telling one another increasingly fantastic stories to pass the time. Mary Shelley produced what would become Frankenstein, and Polidori produced 'The Vampyre'.

Aubrey meets Lord Ruthven, a man of mystery and probably foreign. Aubrey makes a journey with Ruthven to Rome, but then Aubrey travels to Greece on his own where he becomes attracted to Ianthe, an innkeeper's daughter. Ianthe tells Aubrey about the legends of the vampire. Ruthven then arrives, and shortly thereafter Ianthe is killed by a vampire. Aubrey does not connect Ruthven with the murder and the two men continue their travels. They are attacked by bandits and Ruthven is killed. Before he dies, Ruthven makes Aubrey swear an oath that he will not mention his death for a year and a day.

Aubrey goes back to London and is amazed when Ruthven appears, alive and well. Ruthven reminds Aubrey of his oath to keep his death a secret. Ruthven then gets Aubrey's sister to fall in love with him. Aubrey has, by now, worked out that Ruthvin is a source of evil but his oath stops him taking any action.

Ruthven and Aubrey's sister are engaged to marry on the day the oath ends. Aubrey has a nervous breakdown and just before he dies, Aubrey writes a letter to his sister telling her of Ruthven's history, but it does not arrive in time. Ruthven marries Aubrey's sister, kills her on their wedding night, and escapes.

John Polidori died just two years later at the young age of 25. Mary Shelley would later use Polidori as the basis for Dr Frankenstein's assistant in her famous horror story.

Victorian 'Penny dreadfuls'

In Victorian times, most people led hard, dreary lives. They wanted their lives spiced up a bit, and so they read exciting stories. The Gothic Horror story was just right for this time.

Some of Charles Dickens' novels have a Gothic Horror setting, for example 'Oliver Twist' and 'David Copperfield'. Another famous author, Robert Louis Stevenson, wrote the horror story 'The Strange Case of Dr Jekyll and Mr Hyde' in 1886, about a doctor who transformed into a monster.

Some Victorian publishers decided to print horror stories for people to buy cheaply. They were sold for 1p (one penny) and the stories were always of horror and gruesome events spelled out in over-exaggerated ways. As a result, they became known as 'Penny dreadfuls'.

One of the best known stories was 'Varney, the Vampyre; Or, the Feast of Blood' by Thomas Preskett Prest. It was printed as a series of 109 episodes and 220 chapters between 1845 and 1846. The full story was 868 pages long.

The first chapter of this famous story is given on the next pages so that you can read the 'flowery' style that was used in these times.

RNEY THE MPIRE THE

OF BLOOD

CITING INTEREST.

Varney the Vampire; or, The Feast of Blood was a mid-Victorian era Gothic horror story written by James Malcolm Rymer or Thomas Preskett Prest.

The story is set in the 18th century and revolves around the troubles that Sir Francis Varney, a vampire, inflicts upon the Bannerworths, a formerly wealthy family driven to ruin by their recently dead father. Varney hates his condition, but at one point he turns Clara Crofton, a member of another family he terrorises, into a vampire. Varney tries to save himself, but is unable to do so and finally commits suicide by throwing himself into Mount Vesuvius, after having left a written account of his origin with a sympathetic priest.

The Varney story was a big influence on Bram Stoker's 'Dracula', and many of the features we now take for granted were invented in this story: Varney has fangs, leaves two puncture wounds on the necks of his victims, has hypnotic powers, and has superhuman strength. However, unlike later fictional vampires, he is able to go about in daylight and has no particular fear or loathing of crosses or garlic. He can eat and drink in human fashion as a form of disguise, but he points out that human food and drink do not agree with him. His vampirism seems to be a fit that comes on him when his vital energy begins to run low; he is a regular person between feedings.

Varney the Vampyre, Chapter 1

This is the whole of the first chapter.

"How graves give up their dead.

And how the night air hideous grows

With shrieks!"

MIDNIGHT. – THE HAIL-STORM. – THE DREADFUL VISITOR. – THE VAMPYRE.

The solemn tones of an old cathedral clock have announced midnight – the air is thick and heavy – a strange, death like stillness pervades all nature. Like the ominous calm which precedes some more than usually terrific outbreak of the elements, they seem to have paused even in their ordinary fluctuations, to gather a terrific strength for the great effort. A faint peal of thunder now comes from far off. Like a signal gun for the battle of the winds to begin, it appeared to awaken them from their lethargy, and one awful, warring hurricane swept over a whole city, producing more devastation in the four or five minutes it lasted, than would a half century of ordinary phenomena.

It was as if some giant had blown upon some toy town, and scattered many of the buildings before the hot blast of his terrific breath; for as suddenly as that blast of wind had come did it cease, and all was as still and calm as before.

Sleepers awakened, and thought that what they had heard must be the confused chimera of a dream. They trembled and turned to sleep again.

All is still – still as the very grave. Not a sound breaks the magic of repose. What is that – a strange, pattering noise, as of a million of fairy feet? It is hail – yes, a hail-storm has burst over the city. Leaves are dashed from the trees, mingled with small boughs; windows that lie most opposed to the direct fury of the pelting particles of ice are broken, and the rapt repose that before was so remarkable in its intensity, is exchanged for a noise which, in its accumulation, drowns every cry of surprise or consternation which here and there arose from persons who found their houses invaded by the storm.

Now and then, too, there would come a sudden gust of wind that in its strength, as it blew laterally, would, for a moment, hold millions of the hailstones suspended in mid air, but it was only to dash them with redoubled force in some new direction, where more mischief was to be done.

Oh, how the storm raged! Hail – rain – wind. It was, in very truth, an awful night.

There is an antique chamber in an ancient house. Curious and quaint carvings adorn the walls, and the large chimney-piece is a curiosity of itself. The ceiling is low, and a large bay window, from roof to floor, looks to the west. The window is latticed, and filled with curiously painted glass and rich stained pieces, which send in a strange, yet beautiful light, when sun or moon shines into the apartment. There is but one portrait in that room, although the walls seem panelled for the express purpose of containing a series of pictures. That portrait is of a young man, with a pale face, a stately brow, and a strange expression about the eyes, which no one cared to look on twice.

There is a stately bed in that chamber, of carved walnut-wood is it made, rich in design and elaborate in execution; one of those works of art which owe their existence to the Elizabethan era. It is hung with heavy silken and damask furnishing; nodding feathers are at its corners – covered with dust are they, and they lend a funereal aspect to the room. The floor is of polished oak.

God! how the hail dashes on the old bay window! Like an occasional discharge of mimic musketry, it comes clashing, beating, and cracking upon

the small panes; but they resist it – their small size saves them; the wind, the hail, the rain, expend their fury in vain.

The bed in that old chamber is occupied. A creature formed in all fashions of loveliness lies in a half sleep upon that ancient couch – a girl young and beautiful as a spring morning. Her long hair has escaped from its confinement and streams over the blackened coverings of the bedstead; she has been restless in her sleep, for the clothing of the bed is in much confusion. One arm is over her head, the other hangs nearly off the side of the bed near to which she lies. A neck and bosom that would have formed a study for the rarest sculptor that ever Providence gave genius to, were half disclosed. She moaned slightly in her sleep, and once or twice the lips moved as if in prayer – at least one might judge so, for the name of Him who suffered for all came once faintly from them.

She has endured much fatigue, and the storm does not awaken her; but it can disturb the slumbers it does not possess the power to destroy entirely. The turmoil of the elements wakes the senses, although it cannot entirely break the repose they have lapsed into.

Oh, what a world of witchery was in that mouth, slightly parted, and exhibiting within the pearly teeth that glistened even in the faint light that came from that bay window. How sweetly the long silken eyelashes lay upon the cheek. Now she moves, and one shoulder is entirely visible – whiter, fairer than the spotless clothing of the bed on which she lies, is the smooth skin of that fair creature, just budding into womanhood, and in that transition state which presents to us all the charms of the girl – almost of the child, with the more matured beauty and gentleness of advancing years.

Was that lightning? Yes – an awful, vivid, terrifying flash – then a roaring peal of thunder, as if a thousand mountains were rolling one over the other in the blue vault of Heaven! Who sleeps now in that ancient city? Not one living soul. The dread trumpet of eternity could not more effectually have awakened any one.

The hail continues. The wind continues. The uproar of the elements seems at its height. Now she awakens – that beautiful girl on the antique bed; she opens those eyes of celestial blue, and a faint cry of alarm bursts from her lips. At least it is a cry which, amid the noise and turmoil without, sounds but faint and weak. She sits upon the bed and presses her hands upon her eyes. Heavens! what a wild torrent of wind, and rain, and hail! The thunder likewise seems intent upon awakening sufficient echoes to last until the next flash of forked lightning should again produce the wild concussion of the air. She murmurs a prayer – a prayer for those she loves best; the names of those dear to her gentle heart come from her lips; she weeps and prays; she thinks then of what devastation the storm must surely produce, and to the great God of Heaven she prays for all living things. Another flash – a wild, blue, bewildering flash of lightning streams across that bay window, for an instant bringing out every colour in it with terrible distinctness. A shriek bursts from the lips of the young girl, and then, with eyes fixed upon that window, which, in another moment, is all darkness, and with such an expression of terror upon her face as it had never before known, she trembled, and the perspiration of intense fear stood upon her brow.

"What – what was it?" she gasped; "real, or a delusion? Oh, God, what was it? A figure tall and gaunt, endeavouring from the outside to unclasp the window. I saw it. That flash of lightning revealed it to me. It stood the whole length of the window."

There was a lull of the wind. The hail was not falling so thickly – moreover, it now fell, what there was of it, straight, and yet a strange clattering sound came upon the glass of that long window. It could not be a delusion – she is awake, and she hears it. What can produce it? Another flash of lightning – another shriek – there could be now no delusion.

A tall figure is standing on the ledge immediately outside the long window. It is its finger-nails upon the glass that produces the sound so like the hail, now that the hail has ceased. Intense fear paralysed the limbs of that beautiful girl. That one shriek is all she can utter – with hands clasped, a face of marble, a heart beating so wildly in her bosom, that each moment it seems as if it would break its confines, eyes distended and fixed upon the window, she waits, froze with horror. The pattering and clattering of the nails continue. No word is spoken, and now she fancies she can trace the darker form of that figure against the window, and she can see the long arms moving to and fro, feeling for some mode of entrance. What strange light is that which now gradually creeps up into the air? red and terrible – brighter and brighter it grows. The lightning has set fire to a mill, and the reflection of the rapidly consuming building falls upon that long window. There can be no mistake. The figure is there, still feeling for an entrance, and clattering against the glass with its long nails, that appear as if the growth of many years had been untouched. She tries to scream again but a choking sensation comes over her, and she cannot. It is too dreadful – she tries to move – each limb seems weighed down by tons of lead – she can but in a hoarse faint whisper cry, –

"Help – help – help – help!"

And that one word she repeats like a person in a dream. The red glare of the fire continues. It throws up the tall gaunt figure in hideous relief against the long window. It shows, too, upon the one portrait that is in the chamber, and that portrait appears to fix its eyes upon the attempting intruder, while the flickering light from the fire makes it look fearfully lifelike. A small pane of glass is broken, and the form from without introduces a long gaunt hand, which seems utterly destitute of flesh. The fastening is removed, and one-half of the window, which opens like folding doors, is swung wide open upon its hinges.

And yet now she could not scream – she could not move. "Help! – help! – help!" was all she could say. But, oh, that look of terror that sat upon her face, it was dreadful – a look to haunt the memory for a lifetime – a look to obtrude itself upon the happiest moments, and turn them to bitterness.

The figure turns half round, and the light falls upon the face. It is perfectly white – perfectly bloodless. The eyes look like polished tin; the lips are drawn back, and the principal feature next to those dreadful eyes is the teeth – the fearful looking teeth – projecting like those of some wild animal, hideously, glaringly white, and fang-like. It approaches the bed with a strange, gliding movement. It clashes together the long nails that literally appear to hang from the finger ends. No sound comes from its lips. Is she going mad – that young and beautiful girl exposed to so much terror? she has drawn up all her limbs; she cannot even now say help. The power of articulation is gone, but the power of movement has returned to her; she can draw herself slowly along to the other side of the bed from that towards which the hideous appearance is coming.

But her eyes are fascinated. The glance of a serpent could not have produced a greater effect upon her than did the fixed gaze of those awful, metallic-looking eyes that were bent on her face. Crouching down so that the gigantic height was lost, and the horrible, protruding, white face was the most prominent object, came on the figure. What was it? – what did it want there? – what made it look so hideous – so unlike an inhabitant of the earth, and yet to be on it?

Now she has got to the verge of the bed, and the figure pauses. It seemed as if when it paused she lost the power to proceed. The clothing of the bed was now clutched in her hands with unconscious power. She drew her breath short and thick. Her bosom heaves, and her limbs tremble, yet she cannot withdraw her eyes from that marble-looking face. He holds her with his glittering eye.

The storm has ceased – all is still. The winds are hushed; the church clock proclaims the hour of one: a hissing sound comes from the throat of the hideous being, and he raises his long, gaunt arms – the lips move. He advances. The girl places one small foot from the bed on to the floor. She is unconsciously dragging the clothing with her. The door of the room is in that direction – can she reach it? Has she power to walk? – can she withdraw her eyes from the face of the intruder, and so break the hideous charm? God of Heaven! is it real, or some dream so like reality as to nearly overturn the judgment for ever?

The figure has paused again, and half on the bed and half out of it that young girl lies trembling. Her long hair streams across the entire width of the bed. As she has slowly moved along she has left it streaming across the pillows. The pause lasted about a minute – oh, what an age of agony. That minute was, indeed, enough for madness to do its full work in.

With a sudden rush that could not be foreseen – with a strange howling cry that was enough to awaken terror in every breast, the figure seized the long tresses of her hair, and twining them round his bony hands he held her to the bed. Then she screamed – Heaven granted her then power to scream. Shriek followed shriek in rapid succession. The bed-clothes fell in a heap by the side of the bed – she was dragged by her long silken hair completely on to it again. Her beautifully rounded limbs quivered with the agony of her soul. The glassy, horrible eyes of the figure ran over that angelic form with a hideous satisfaction – horrible profanation. He drags her head to the bed's edge. He forces it back by the long hair still entwined in his grasp. With a plunge he seizes her neck in his fang-like teeth – a gush of blood, and a hideous sucking noise follows. The girl has swooned, and the vampyre is at his hideous repast!... (the rest of this story can be found at www.gutenberg.org)

Victorian melodrama

To cater for the mood of the times, a very special kind of play was also developed, often based on horror stories. It was called the melodrama.

The term melodrama means a dramatic work which exaggerates plot and characters in order to appeal to the emotions. It is made of the words *melos*, meaning music, and *dram*, meaning a play. In Victorian times, the sense of fear was made greater by the use of creepy music. Exactly the same idea is used in horror movies today.

In a music hall and in most popular theatres, the audience was encouraged to be part of the performance. So everything had to be simple and all the characters had to be easily understood by the audience.

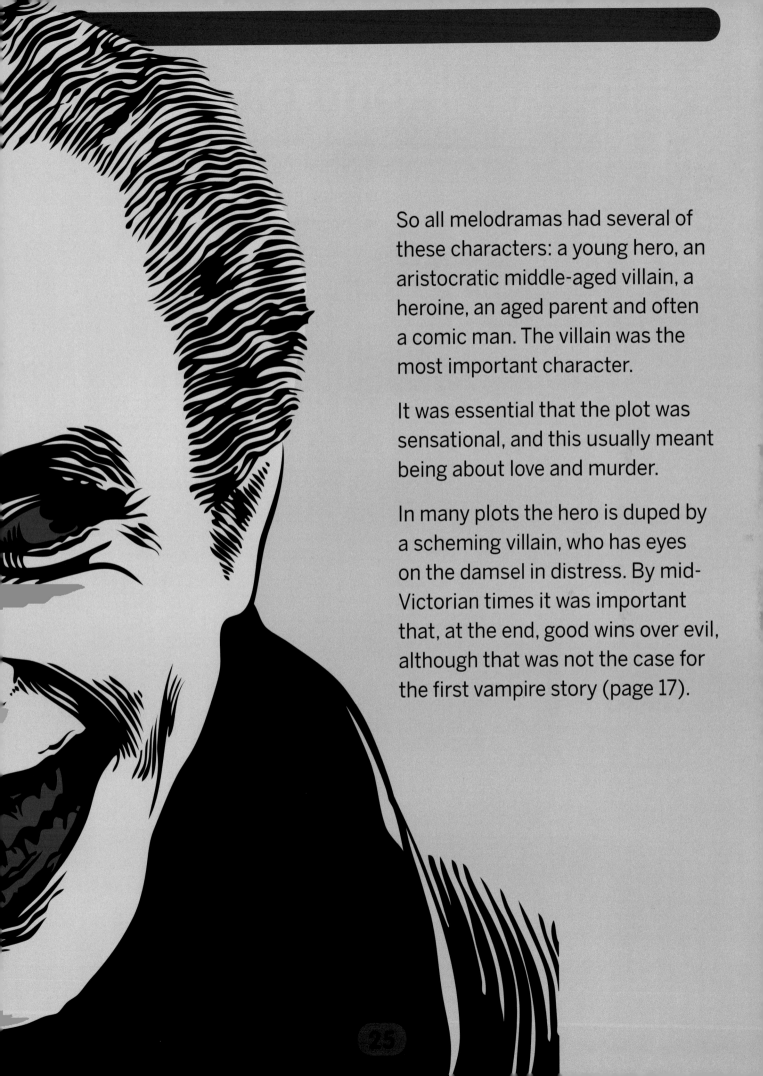

So all melodramas had several of these characters: a young hero, an aristocratic middle-aged villain, a heroine, an aged parent and often a comic man. The villain was the most important character.

It was essential that the plot was sensational, and this usually meant being about love and murder.

In many plots the hero is duped by a scheming villain, who has eyes on the damsel in distress. By mid-Victorian times it was important that, at the end, good wins over evil, although that was not the case for the first vampire story (page 17).

Bram Stoker and 'Dracula'

'Dracula' is the most famous vampire story ever written. It was written by Bram Stoker, who was an Irishman born in 1847.

Stoker was a newspaper editor, but he was attracted to the theatre, and eventually became manager of the famous touring company whose star was the Shakespearian actor Henry Irving.

It was in 1897, while working for Henry Irving, that he began writing 'Dracula'.

This was no spur-of-the-moment story, but rather it was very carefully researched. Over several years Stoker read up all he could on Eastern European folklore and stories of vampires. His intention was to make the whole story seem as real as possible, because, in this way, it would be all the more frightening.

The story he finally wrote is in the form of a collection of realistic, but completely fictional, diary entries, telegrams, letters, ship's logs, and newspaper clippings. By telling the same tale from different perspectives the reader starts to think 'they can't all be lying', there is no smoke without fire, and once the seeds of reality are sown, the true horror of the story begins to grip the reader.

Stoker's book was influenced by reading about Eastern European folklore, and especially stories from Transylvania, places he had been, such as Whitby in Yorkshire and Slains Castle in Aberdeenshire, as well as stories that had already been written, such as 'Carmilla' by Joseph Sheridan Le Fanu. He also read 'The Land Beyond the Forest ' by Emily Gerard and other books about Transylvania and vampires. However, it was in London that a colleague told him the story of Vlad the Impaler whose name was Dracula, and Stoker immediately added this to his book.

Bram Stoker used to work for one of the best-known Shakespearian actors of Victorian times – Henry Irving. It is said that Stoker based the character of Count Dracula on the mannerisms of Henry Irving. Stoker wanted Irving to play the part of Dracula in a stage play – but he never agreed. Many other people have played Dracula since, however, one of the most famous was Christopher Lee.

Dracula

The tale begins with Jonathan Harker travelling to Count Dracula's crumbling, remote castle in the Carpathian Mountains in Transylvania. He goes there to complete a house purchase. At first he is charmed by Dracula's gracious manner, but then Harker finds he has become a prisoner in the castle. He also begins to discover strange things about what Count Dracula does at night. Harker then falls under the spell of three female vampires, the Brides of Dracula, but eventually escapes from the castle.

Harker knows that Count Dracula wants to go to England to be among the 'teeming millions'. Not long afterward, a Russian ship runs aground on the shores of Whitby, during a storm. The captain's log tells of strange events that had taken place during the ship's journey in which the entire crew disappear one by one. A large dog is seen leaping ashore from the ship, and the ship's cargo is found to contain boxes of earth from Transylvania.

Now Dracula seeks out Harker's fiancée, Wilhelmina 'Mina' Murray, and her friend, Lucy Westenra. Meanwhile one of Mina's friends, a Doctor Seward's patient called Renfield, wants to eat insects, spiders, birds, and other creatures in order to soak up their 'life force'. Renfield is used to locate Dracula.

Then Lucy begins to waste away. Seward calls in his old teacher, Professor Abraham Van Helsing from Amsterdam. Van Helsing knows the cause of Lucy's condition but refuses to tell them what it is. Van Helsing tries multiple blood transfusions, but they do not work. Then Lucy and her mother are attacked by a wolf. Mrs Westenra, who has a heart condition, dies of fright, and Lucy apparently dies soon after.

Lucy is buried, but soon afterward the newspapers report children being stalked in the night 'by a beautiful lady'. Van Helsing, knowing that this means Lucy has become a vampire, tells

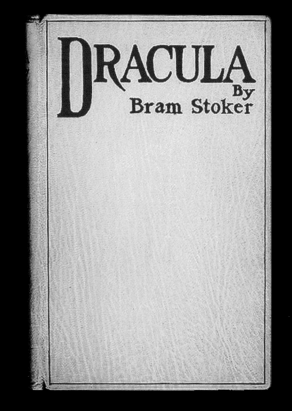

Seward. They track her down, stake her heart, behead her, and fill her mouth with garlic.

Jonathan Harker arrives home from Budapest (where Mina joined and married him after his escape from the castle); he and Mina also join the others, who must now defeat Dracula.

After Dracula learns of Van Helsing and the others plotting against him, he takes revenge by visiting – and biting – Mina at least three times. Dracula also feeds Mina his blood, creating a bond between them so that he can control her. The only way to stop this is to kill Dracula.

Mina slowly falls under the spell of the vampire and becomes telepathically connected with Dracula. It is this connection that they start to use to find Dracula's movements.

Dracula flees back to his castle in Transylvania, followed by Van Helsing's group, who manage to track him down just before sundown, and kill him by stabbing him in the heart. Dracula crumbles to dust, his spell is lifted and Mina is freed from the vampire's spell.

Dracula, Chapter 1

This is the whole of the first chapter.

[This is an abridged version]

3 May.

Having had some time at my disposal when in London, I had visited the British Museum, and made search among the books and maps in the library regarding Transylvania; it had struck me that some foreknowledge of the country could hardly fail to have some importance in dealing with a nobleman of that country.

I find that the district he named is in the extreme east of the country, just on the borders of three states, Transylvania, Moldavia, and Bukovina, in the midst of the Carpathian mountains; one of the wildest and least known portions of Europe.

I was not able to light on any map or work giving the exact locality of the Castle Dracula, as there are no maps of this country as yet to compare with our own Ordnance Survey Maps; but I found that Bistritz, the post town named by Count Dracula, is a fairly well-known place.

I did not sleep well, though my bed was comfortable enough, for I had all sorts of queer dreams. There was a dog howling all night under my window, which may have had something to do with it; or it may have been the paprika, for I had to drink up all the water in my carafe, and was still thirsty. Towards morning I slept and was wakened by the continuous knocking at my door, so I guess I must have been sleeping soundly then.

I had to hurry breakfast, for the train started a little before eight, or rather it ought to have done so, for after rushing to the station at 7:30 I had to sit in the carriage for more than an hour before we began to move.

All day long we seemed to dawdle through a country which was full of beauty of every kind. It was on the dark side of twilight when we got to Bistritz, which is a very interesting old place. Count Dracula had directed me to go to the Golden Krone Hotel, which I found, to my great delight, to be thoroughly old-fashioned, for of course I wanted to see all I could of the ways of the country.

I was evidently expected, for when I got near the door I faced a cheery-looking elderly woman in the usual peasant dress. When I came close she bowed and said, "The Herr Englishman?"

"Yes," I said, "Jonathan Harker."

She smiled, and gave some message to an elderly man in white shirtsleeves, who had followed her to the door.

He went, but immediately returned with a letter:

"My friend. – Welcome to the Carpathians. I am anxiously expecting you. Sleep well tonight. I trust that your journey from London has been a happy one, and that you will enjoy your stay in my beautiful land. – Your friend, Dracula."

I found that my landlord had got a letter from the Count, directing him to secure the best place

on the coach for me. Just before I was leaving, the old lady came up to my room and said in a hysterical way: "Must you go? Oh! Young Herr, must you go?"

"It is the eve of St. George's Day. Do you not know that tonight, when the clock strikes midnight, all the evil things in the world will have full sway? Do you know where you are going, and what you are going to?" She was in such evident distress that I tried to comfort her, but without effect. Finally, she went down on her knees and implored me not to go; at least to wait a day or two before starting.

She then rose and dried her eyes, and taking a crucifix from her neck offered it to me. She saw, I suppose, the doubt in my face, for she put the rosary round my neck and said, "For your mother's sake," and went out of the room.

I am writing up this part of the diary whilst I am waiting for the coach, which is, of course, late; and the crucifix is still round my neck.

Whether it is the old lady's fear, or the many ghostly traditions of this place, or the crucifix itself, I do not know, but I am not feeling nearly as easy in my mind as usual.

I must say [the local people] were not cheering to me, for amongst [the words they were using] were "Ordog" – Satan, "Pokol" – hell, "stregoica" – witch, "vrolok" and "vlkoslak" – both mean the same thing, one being Slovak and the other Servian for something that is either werewolf or vampire.

When we started, the crowd round the inn door, which had by this time swelled to a considerable size, all made the sign of the cross and pointed two fingers towards me.

With some difficulty, I got a fellow passenger to tell me what they meant. He would not answer at first, but on learning that I was English, he explained that it was a charm or guard against the evil eye.

This was not very pleasant for me, just starting for an unknown place to meet an unknown man. But everyone seemed so kind-hearted, and so sorrowful, and so sympathetic that I could not but be touched.

Beyond the green swelling hills of the Mittel Land rose mighty slopes of forest up to the lofty steeps of the Carpathians themselves. Right and left of us they towered, with the afternoon sun falling full upon them and bringing out all the glorious colours of this beautiful range, deep blue and purple in the shadows of the peaks, green and brown where grass and rock mingled, and an endless perspective of jagged rock and pointed crags, till these were themselves lost in the distance, where the snowy peaks rose grandly.

As the evening fell it began to get very cold, and the growing twilight seemed to merge into one dark mistiness the gloom of the trees, oak, beech, and pine, though in the valleys which ran deep between the spurs of the hills, as we ascended through the Pass, the dark firs stood out here and there against the background of late-lying snow. Sometimes, as the road was cut through the pine woods that seemed in the darkness to be closing down upon us, great masses of greyness which here and there bestrewed the trees, produced a peculiarly weird and solemn effect, which carried on the thoughts and grim fancies engendered earlier in the evening, when the falling sunset threw into strange relief the ghost-like clouds which amongst the Carpathians seem to wind ceaselessly through the valleys. Sometimes the hills were so steep that, despite our driver's haste, the horses could only go slowly. I wished to get down and walk up them, as we do at home, but the driver would not hear of it. "No, no," he said. "You must not walk here. The dogs are too fierce." And then he added, with what he evidently meant for grim pleasantry – for he looked round to catch the approving smile of the rest – "And you may have enough of such matters before you go to sleep." The only stop he would make was a moment's pause to light his lamps.

I was now myself looking out for the conveyance which was to take me to the Count. Each moment I expected to see the glare of lamps through the blackness, but all was dark. Then, amongst a chorus of screams from the peasants

and a universal crossing of themselves, a caleche, with four horses, drove up behind us, overtook us, and drew up beside the coach. I could see from the flash of our lamps as the rays fell on them, that the horses were coal-black and splendid animals. They were driven by a tall man, with a long brown beard and a great black hat, which seemed to hide his face from us. I could only see the gleam of a pair of very bright eyes, which seemed red in the lamplight, as he turned to us.

Without a word he shook his reins, the horses turned, and we swept into the darkness of the pass. By-and-by, however, as I was curious to know how time was passing, I struck a match, and by its flame looked at my watch. It was within a few minutes of midnight. This gave me a sort of shock, for I suppose the general superstition about midnight was increased by my recent experiences. I waited with a sick feeling of suspense.

Then a dog began to howl somewhere in a farmhouse far down the road, a long, agonized wailing, as if from fear. The sound was taken up by another dog, and then another and another, till, borne on the wind which now sighed softly through the Pass, a wild howling began, which seemed to come from all over the country, as far as the imagination could grasp it through the gloom of the night.

Soon we were hemmed in with trees, which in places arched right over the roadway till we passed as through a tunnel. And again great frowning rocks guarded us boldly on either side. Though we were in shelter, we could hear the rising wind, for it moaned and whistled through the rocks, and the branches of the trees crashed together as we swept along. It grew colder and colder still, and fine, powdery snow began to fall, so that soon we and all around us were covered with a white blanket. The keen wind still carried the howling of the dogs, though this grew fainter as we went on our way. The baying of the wolves sounded nearer and nearer, as though they were closing round on us from every side. I grew dreadfully afraid, and the horses shared my fear. The driver, however, was not in the least disturbed. He kept turning his head to left and right, but I could not see anything through the darkness.

We kept on ascending, with occasional periods of quick descent, but in the main always ascending. Suddenly, I became conscious of the fact that the driver was in the act of pulling up the horses in the courtyard of a vast ruined castle, from whose tall black windows came no ray of light, and whose broken battlements showed a jagged line against the sky... (the rest of this story can be found at www.gutenberg.org)

Dracula and Transylvania

Count Dracula is from Transylvania. Transylvania is in the wooded Carpathian mountains, a region in the north of Romania.

It is one of the remotest parts of Europe and is very difficult to cross because of its many deep valleys.

It was one of the places to hold out against the Ancient Romans, although it eventually became the province of Dacia.

When the Romans left, it split up into small independent kingdoms, whose lands were defended by castles placed on high, rocky pinnacles overlooking the main valleys.

Dracula's home: Bran

The supposed home of Count Dracula in Transylvania is Castle Bran. How can this distant place be connected to an English writer who never visited Romania?

Castle Bran began as a simple wooden fortress in 1212. It was later rebuilt in stone on its high crag.

It became famous as the base used by Vlad the Impaler when he was attacking Transylvania. His cruel deeds and extraordinary life were recorded by many historians.

Vlad was the inspiration for Count Dracula and his exploits were in the books that Bram Stoker would have read during his researches into Transylvania.

Today Castle Bran is a museum.

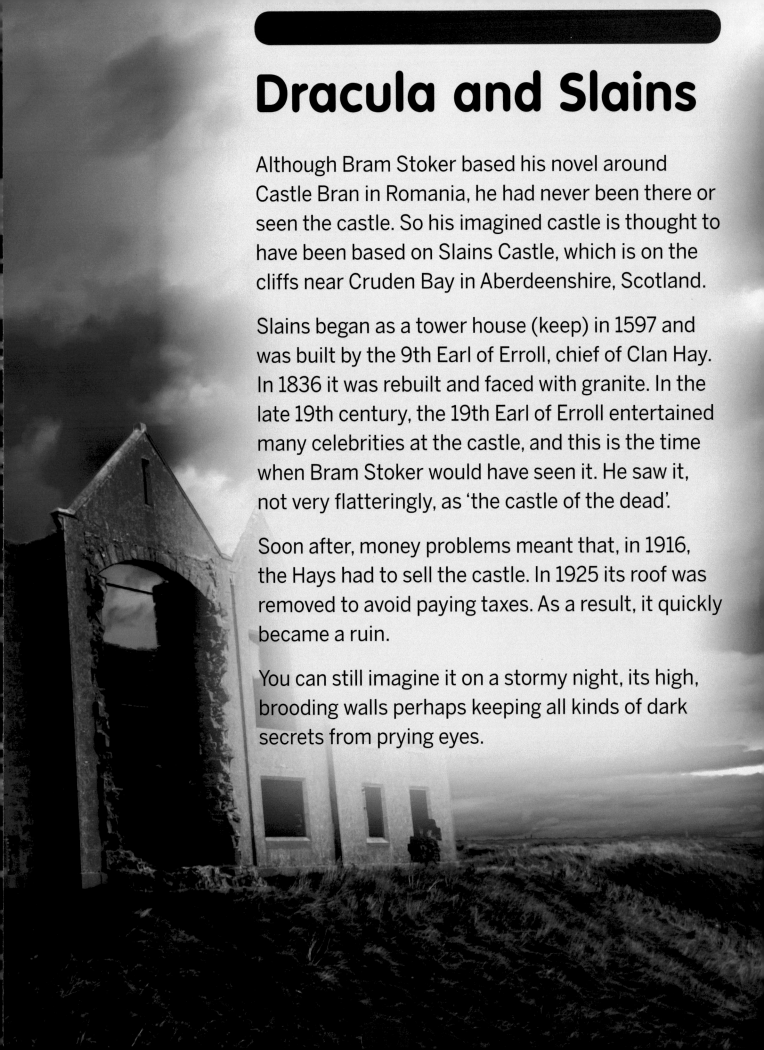

Dracula and Slains

Although Bram Stoker based his novel around Castle Bran in Romania, he had never been there or seen the castle. So his imagined castle is thought to have been based on Slains Castle, which is on the cliffs near Cruden Bay in Aberdeenshire, Scotland.

Slains began as a tower house (keep) in 1597 and was built by the 9th Earl of Erroll, chief of Clan Hay. In 1836 it was rebuilt and faced with granite. In the late 19th century, the 19th Earl of Erroll entertained many celebrities at the castle, and this is the time when Bram Stoker would have seen it. He saw it, not very flatteringly, as 'the castle of the dead'.

Soon after, money problems meant that, in 1916, the Hays had to sell the castle. In 1925 its roof was removed to avoid paying taxes. As a result, it quickly became a ruin.

You can still imagine it on a stormy night, its high, brooding walls perhaps keeping all kinds of dark secrets from prying eyes.

Dracula and Whitby

Bram Stoker stayed in a house in the seaside port of Whitby, North Yorkshire, and while there he visited the public library and obtained a book about the legends of Transylvania.

In the story Count Dracula has to find a way of getting to England. But no one knows that. Not long afterward, a Russian ship arriving from Eastern Europe, runs aground near Whitby during a fierce storm. Only the captain is found, and he is dead. The captain's log tells of strange events during the ship's journey with all the crew disappearing one by one due to an evil presence on board the ship.

Then a large dog is seen leaping ashore from the stricken ship. The ship's cargo is silver sand – and boxes of earth from Transylvania.

Dracula and Vlad the Impaler

Bram Stoker wrote a number of sensational novels because they paid well. So he was always on the lookout for gruesome people to give some historical background. For Dracula he found the story of Vlad III the Impaler.

Vlad III was Prince of Wallachia and ruled part of Transylvania between 1456 and 1462. The British King at the time was Henry VI. He was murdered in the Tower of London. This was the time of the Wars of the Roses, so, as you can see, these were pretty violent times all over Europe.

In Transylvania, Vlad was faced with a problem: the invasion of the Turks. Vlad was, indeed, called Dracula. In Romanian it means "Son of the dragon". His father was Vlad Dracul, who had joined the Order of the Dragon. At the age of five, young Vlad was also initiated into the Order.

Vlad III, the Impaler.

Then things became complicated. When Vlad III was a boy, his father needed help to keep his throne, and he got that from the Turks on condition he paid tribute to the Turks. In order to secure his service, Vlad II had to send his sons to Turkey as hostages. At eleven years of age, Vlad III was imprisoned and often whipped and beaten because of his verbal abuse towards his captors and his stubborn behaviour. These early years led to Vlad III's hatred for the Turks. He also distrusted his own father for trading him to the Turks and betraying the Order of the Dragon's oath to fight them.

Then a revolt in Transylvania led to the murder of Vlad II and Vlad III's brother. The Turks put Vlad III on the throne, but the land was soon invaded and Vlad III had to flee west.

Then the Turks began to spread their empire west and Vlad III led one of the armies that opposed them.

On September 26, 1459, Pope Pius II called for a new crusade against the Turks, and although most countries did not send troops, Vlad III was enthusiastic and to provoke the Turks, Vlad had Turkish representatives killed, by nailing their turbans to their heads. Vlad now had a crusading lust. He wrote "I have killed men and women, old and young... 23,884 Turks and Bulgarians without counting those whom we burned alive in their homes or whose heads were not chopped off by our soldiers..." When the Sultan sent an army, they found 20,000 Turkish soldiers impaled along the route.

Vlad had not secured his throne, and he was deposed twice. His third reign lasted two months and this time he was killed by the Turks who decapitated his corpse, preserved his head in honey and sent it to the Sultan who had it displayed on a stake as proof that the Impaler was finally dead.

No one knows how many people he had killed during his lifetime, but it may have been as many as 100,000.

It is most likely that Bram Stoker found the name for his vampire from a book he read about these times. The cruel history of the Impaler was just right for Stoker's story.

Stories of vampires are a feature of legends in Eastern Europe. During the 17th century travellers returning from the Balkans brought with them tales of the undead and, as a result, authors and playwrights began to explore the vampire legend. Stoker's novel was the best of a long series of works that were inspired by the reports coming from the Balkans and Hungary.

So now you can see how legends of vampires, cruel princes and impalement all came together in his story. Dracula thus became a natural person to describe as a vampire.

Vampire bats

Vampire bats are real. Their front teeth are specialized for cutting skin, and their saliva contains a substance, draculin, which prevents the prey's blood from clotting. The vampire bats do not, however, suck blood, but rather lap the blood where they have cut the skin of their prey using their sharp teeth. As this is done at night, the prey may not even be aware of it because they stay asleep. The common vampire bat feeds on the blood of mammals, including people. The signs of a bat having sucked blood are two parallel cut marks in the skin. So here is the origin of the two-prong bite mark on the skin of a vampire's victim.

Bats that lick blood (and now named vampire bats) live only in South America. The idea of bats being connected to vampires is quite recent. This is because there are no blood-sucking bats in Europe and their addition to the story had to wait for the blood-licking species to be found in South America. Of course, it did not take long for them to be described as vampire bats.

Bram Stoker used the relationship between a bat (which only flies at night), the vampire bat (which cuts its victim and then licks the blood) and his Count Dracula to make Dracula change into a bat several times and so arrive unexpectedly, or to get away from danger.

To make it possible for Dracula to bite his victim, he needed fangs. Fangs and hate of sunlight are both 19th century additions to the legend. Hence Count Dracula had protruding teeth. Stoker's Dracula did not have a cloak: that appeared in order to add drama to plays in the 1920s.

Vampires and Halloween

When it comes round to Halloween, many children dress up as vampires. So what is the connection?

Halloween is based on ancient customs, especially Celtic ones. Evenings are drawing in and nights are long. The creepiness of darkness is upon us. The Celtic festival that we now call Halloween may be based on the Celtic festival of Samhain, or summer's end, where night is longer than day, when the harvest has been gathered. Celtic peoples believed that this was the

time of year when spirits could enter or pass through the living world. Some of these spirits, such as ancestors, were good spirits, but it was also a time when evil spirits could enter the world as well. These evil spirits had to be kept away by wearing costumes and masks. People disguised themselves as evil spirits in order to keep other evil spirits away. Many of these rituals took place around bonfires.

The word Halloween comes from the Old English All-Hallows-Eve, that is, the night before All Hallows Day. All Hallows Eve is followed by All Saints Day which celebrates all saints, known and unknown. The day after is All Souls Day, which celebrates the departed faithful who have not yet reached heaven. So, as you can see, this is a very powerful time of year now as well as in the past. Christians believe there is a spirit connection between the living and the dead. Those who have died and are with God watch over those still living, with the saints helping the living on behalf of God.

The close connection between these days meant that, in Medieval times, souls who had not yet reached heaven (and were in purgatory) were remembered with a candlelit festival. Turnips were carved out, candles placed inside the turnips and used as lanterns. The sides of the lanterns were carved with faces, the idea being to ward off evil spirits. They were then placed in windows or on doorsteps after dark. In North America, pumpkins can be grown, and these are larger than parsnips, and so pumpkins have now become the symbol of Halloween.

During Victorian times, the ideas of melodrama and Gothic horror became intermingled with Halloween, and so the images of Halloween are now not just pumpkins, but themes of death, evil, the occult, magic, or mythical monsters: ghosts, witches, skeletons, vampires, werewolves, demons, bats, and black cats.

Halloween costumes were also a Victorian invention, and are of monsters, ghosts, skeletons, witches, and devils. Nowadays, telling of ghost stories and viewing of horror films are all part of Halloween parties. New horror films are often released just before the holiday to take advantage of the atmosphere.

Be a vampire

It is good fun to dress up as a vampire. As you know, the idea of the vampire, what he wears and what he does, have all changed since the first vampire book was written two centuries ago. The vampire has slicked back hair, sunken eyes, a white (dead) complexion, a nobleman's cloak and other clothes. The inside of the cloak is blood red to match the blood around his mouth. And the finishing touch is a good set of fangs. Here the vampire is seen with another dress up character – the grim reaper (death).

Write a vampire story

You can make up many kinds of stories involving vampires. Here are pictures of your two main characters. Now what story can you write of them?

Curriculum Visions

Curriculum Visions Explorers

Explorers make complicated subjects simple. They guide you one picture at a time, so you can learn the important facts in an orderly and easy way. No other book makes learning so easy and enjoyable.

A CVP Book
Copyright © 2011 Atlantic Europe Publishing

The right of Brian Knapp to be identified as the author of this work has been asserted by him in accordance with the Copyright, Designs and Patents Act 1988.

All rights reserved. No part of this publication may be reproduced, stored in a retrieval system, or transmitted in any form or by any means, electronic, mechanical, photocopying, recording or otherwise, without prior permission of the copyright holder.

Author
Brian Knapp, BSc, PhD

Senior Designer
Adele Humphries, BA

Editor
Gillian Gatehouse

Photographs
Earthscape and Shutterstock Picture Libraries, except the following: *TopFoto* pages 18–19, 27 (inset) and 42.

Designed and produced by
Atlantic Europe Publishing

Printed in China by
WKT Company Ltd

Vampires from Vampyre to Dracula
– Curriculum Visions
A CIP record for this book is available from the British Library
ISBN 978 1 86214 675 4

This product is manufactured from sustainable managed forests. For every tree cut down at least one more is planted.